Half Yard
Vintage

Half Yard
Vintage
Debbie Shore

**Sew 23 gorgeous accessories
from left-over pieces of fabric**

SEARCH PRESS

First published in 2017

Search Press Limited
Wellwood, North Farm Road,
Tunbridge Wells, Kent TN2 3DR

Photographs by Garie Hind

Text copyright © Debbie Shore 2017
Photographs © Garie Hind 2017
Design copyright © Search Press Ltd. 2017

ISBN: 978-1-78221-458-8

The Publishers and author can accept no
responsibility for any consequences arising from
the information, advice or instructions given in
this publication.

Readers are permitted to rep
items/patterns in this book fo
use, or for the purpose of se
of charge and without the pr
the Publishers. Any use of th
commercial purposes is not
the prior permission of the P

For further inspiration, visit D
channel: www.youtube.com

Suppliers
For details of suppliers, please visit the
Search Press website: www.searchpress.com

Printed in China by 1010 Printing International Ltd

Acknowledgements

As this book is about all that is vintage
and nostalgic I've been thinking about
the family members whose creativity I
have been influenced by. My Grandma
and her little knitted teddies, which I
still have (see below); my Mum with her
sewing, tatting (see below) and beautiful
poetry; her sister, just 'Auntie', was an
amazing artist; my Dad, whose skills in
mechanics taught me to figure out how
things are made; and finally my sister
Amanda, who is talented in all of the
above! We have a whole new generation
of grandsons and granddaughters
between us now, and I fully intend to
pass on all of these skills!

Contents

Pillow Cover,
page 18

Posy Cone,
page 20

Jar Wraps,
page 22

Notebook Cover,
page 38

Letter Holder,
page 40

Floral Wreath,
page 44

Dressing Table Mat,
page 48

Doily Clutch,
page 66

Shabby Chic Christmas
Stocking, page 70

Little Cottages,
page 74

Tea Cosy,
page 78

Tray Mat,
page 24

Bunting,
page 28

Bucket Bag,
page 30

Tissuebox Cover,
page 34

Glasses Case,
page 52

Birdhouse Peg Bag,
page 54

Hanging Hearts,
page 58

Shabby Chic Advent
Calendar, page 62

Cake Frill,
page 82

Repair Kit,
page 84

Pincushion Pot,
page 88

Shabby Chic Shoulder Bag,
page 92

Introduction

Natural fabrics like cotton and linen, embroidery and lace, silk ribbons and buttons made from shells are some of the things that remind me of my childhood – delving into the dressing-up box that was kept in the attic, overflowing with fabrics, scarves and too-big-for-me shoes that made me feel very grand!

For the projects in this book I've tried to recreate those nostalgic times but with a modern twist. I've used vintage-inspired fabrics and lace to create purposeful or decorative items for the home – including projects perfect for an afternoon tea such as a tea cosy (see page 78), a cake frill (see page 82) and a beautiful made-to-measure tray mat (see page 24). I've also included plenty of other items that you'll want to keep for yourself or give as gifts – for example, a sweet clutch bag made from doilies (see page 66) or a beautiful pillow cover (see page 18). Finally, there are a few items that will make for a fantastically vintage Christmas: a stocking (see page 70), a wreath (see page 44) and an advent calendar (see page 62). Use a ¼in (5mm) seam allowance unless otherwise stated.

Auction websites and charity shops are a good resource for real vintage lace doilies, beads and buttons, and many modern fabrics have a vintage look to them. And who knows – maybe you'll find a stash of silk scarves, beads, old clothes and fabrics in the dressing-up box in your attic!

Debbie x

Sewing kit

SEWING MACHINE

Although vintage sewing machines are lovely pieces of engineering, a modern machine will be much lighter and easier to use. For the projects in this book you won't need anything too fancy, but if you're buying for the first time I'd always recommend a simple computerised machine. Look for a needle up/down facility and the ability to drop the feed dogs if you want to do a little free-motion embroidery – some machines even come equipped with a speed control on board so that you don't need to use the foot pedal.

HAND-SEWING NEEDLES

There will always be a bit of hand sewing in your projects, from sewing turning gaps closed to embroidering decorative stitches, so it's advisable to have a collection of different sized needles. I use a leather thimble to help stop the needle from slipping, or indeed from making my finger sore!

THREADS

Although you probably don't need as many as I do (see opposite), a good selection of threads means you will always have the right colour for the job. Choose a good-quality thread to help create strong seams.

PINS

Keep a few in different sizes. I tend to use glass-headed pins as they are easy to spot if I drop one!

CUTTING TOOLS

A 45mm rotary cutter, 24in (61cm) ruler and large mat are well worth the investment, as you'll enjoy fast and accurate cutting every time. But you'll still need scissors. Use dressmaking shears for fabric; small scissors are good for snipping the ends of threads; pinking shears give a decorative edge to non-woven fabrics like felt and help to stop woven fabrics from fraying. And don't forget to keep one pair of scissors just for paper – paper can damage your fabric shears.

TAPE MEASURE

Never use a fabric tape measure as it can stretch over time. Plastic types may not be the best looking but they are the most accurate.

QUICK UNPICK

You'll usually get one of these supplied with your sewing machine, and you'll need it to unpick the odd wonky stitch. It will blunt after a while, so replace it if it stops cutting smoothly.

MARKING PENS

Pens can be air-, water- or heat-erasable. Remember not to apply heat to air- or water-erasable ink pens as the ink can become permanent. Chalks and pencils are another good option and are available in light or dark colours to stand out against any fabric.

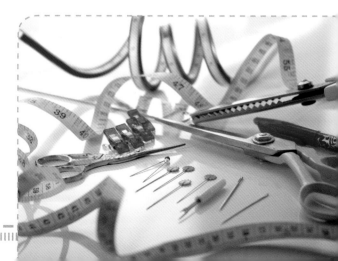

TWEEZERS

For turning out small projects, pushing out corners or using toy filler, you'll find tweezers really useful. They can also be useful for positioning items when gluing, and will keep your fingers from getting sticky!

TRIMMINGS

I like to keep a stash of ribbons, buttons, bias binding (see below) and trimmings so that I always have the perfect embellishment for my projects!

ADHESIVES

Temporary adhesives are a perfect alternative to pinning, particularly for projects with appliqué. Either in spray or stick form, these glues allow you to reposition the fabrics, as they don't form a permanent bond. Permanent adhesives come in many guises: sprays and powders are activated by the heat of an iron; wet glues take a little while to set, allowing you time to manoeuvre if needed. Hot glue guns provide quick-setting, strong glues, but be warned – the glue is very hot as it comes out of the gun!

FABRICS

For advice on choosing vintage-style fabrics and trimmings, see page 17. Here are a few tips to get you started to make sure you get the best results:

- Many fabrics nowadays are pre-shrunk, but if you're not sure, wash and dry your fabric before cutting it.

- Take your time measuring and cutting fabric. If your stitching is wrong you can always unpick it, but if you cut your fabric wrong it could cost you more fabric.

- Change your machine needle after about eight hours of sewing; a blunt needle can pucker your fabric.

- Ironing is an important part of sewing. Your seams will sit better and you'll have a more professional finish if you iron them as you go. Pre-ironed fabric is easier to work with.

- The seam allowance is the distance sewn from the edge of the fabric. For the projects in this book I've allowed ¼in (5mm) unless stated otherwise.

Before you start

Machine stitches

STRAIGHT STITCH

This is the most used stitch on any project. Lengthen the thread to create a tacking/basting stitch. If you loosen the tension, it's easy to pull the bottom thread to gather your fabric.

TRIPLE STRAIGHT STITCH

This stitch won't crack when used on stretch fabric, and it makes a bold outline when used as a decorative stitch.

ZIGZAG STITCH

A decorative stitch that can be used to join two pieces of fabric together to create a flat seam, this stitch can also be useful to help stop the raw edges of your fabric from fraying. Shorten the length of the stitch to make a satin stitch – perfect for edging appliqué shapes.

OVER-EDGE STITCH

This is designed to take the thread slightly over the raw edge of your fabric to stop it from fraying (it is similar to an overlock stitch, which is produced by an overlocker/serger). Use this on items that may wear or need to be laundered; if you sell your items this will give them a professional finish.

DECORATIVE STITCHES

The number of decorative stitches varies from machine to machine, depending on manufacturer and price point. These stitches make pretty borders and finishing touches to your projects, or can simply be embroidered onto ribbon or tape to make embellishments such as bows.

Hand stitches

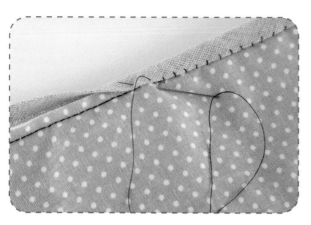

SLIP STITCH

I use this to finish off bias binding (see page 15). Keep the stitch to a short length and try to just catch a couple of strands of the fold of the bias binding to keep the stitch as invisible as possible.

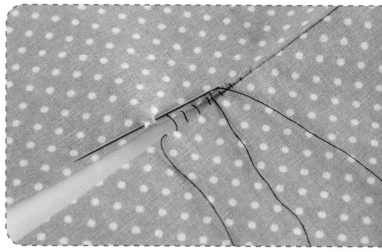

LADDER STITCH

The perfect stitch for closing turning gaps or making repairs in seams: take the needle from one side of the opening to the opposite side, then gently pull to close the gap. Small stitches become the least visible.

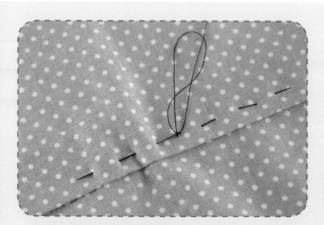

RUNNING STITCH

Use this in the same way as a machine straight stitch. It can be used as a tacking/basting stitch, and the stitches can be pulled to gather the fabric. If tiny, the stitches can be as strong as machined stitches.

BLANKET STITCH

This stitch gives a lovely hand-made look to your projects, works well with felt and really stands out when embroidery thread is used.

CHAIN OR DAISY STITCH

For this decorative embroidery stitch, take the thread around the needle to form a loop, then make one small stitch over the top of the loop to secure. Sew a row to form a chain stitch, or join six loops together in the centre and you have a daisy!

Cutting into curves

For curves that are to be turned, make little 'v'-shaped cuts into the fabric up to the seam – this will stop the fabric from puckering when turned. You could also use pinking shears for the same effect.

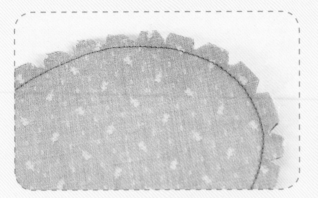

Cutting corners

This helps to keep the corners square when turned the right way out. Cut away the corner, keeping as close to the stitches as you can without snipping them.

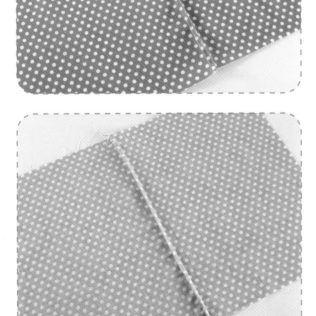

Making French seams

This seam will conceal raw edges of fabric in unlined projects, and is often used with fine fabrics and organza.

1 Sew your fabrics wrong sides together. Trim the seam allowance to ⅛in (3mm).

2 Fold the fabric over the seam right sides together. Sew with a ¼in (5mm) seam allowance, trapping the raw edges in the centre. Open out and press.

3 You will have a neat seam with no raw edges showing from either side.

Making bias binding

Bias tape is a strip of fabric cut on the diagonal, at a 45-degree angle. Cutting on the bias allows a little 'give', so the fabric can stretch around curves without puckering. You can buy it ready-made, but making it yourself allows you to pick the fabric to match your project.

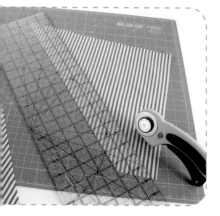

1 To create 1in (2.5cm) wide tape you'll need to cut strips of fabric that are 2in (5cm) wide.

2 To join the strips together, lay two pieces right sides together, overlapping at right angles. Draw a diagonal line across the join from one corner to the other, as in the photograph. Pin the strip together, then sew across this line.

3 Trim the raw edge back to around ⅛in (3mm) and press the seam open.

4 Making bias binding involves folding over both long edges of the tape into the centre and pressing. The easiest way to do this is to use either a bias binding machine or a small bias tape maker (shown), through which you thread the tape. The tape maker folds the strip in two – you press with your iron while pulling the fabric through.

Applying bias binding

1 To apply the binding, first open up the crease lines and fold over the end: crease this with your fingers. Right sides together, pin along the raw edge of your work. Sew with your machine along the crease mark, all the way around your project, and when you come back to the beginning, overlap the binding by about ½in (1cm).

2 Now fold the tape over the raw edge, and use a slip stitch to sew by hand on the back of the piece. An alternative is to top-stitch from the front with your machine, but bear in mind that these stitches will be seen so you'll need to sew a really straight line! If the binding is attached around a curve, it will stretch easily.

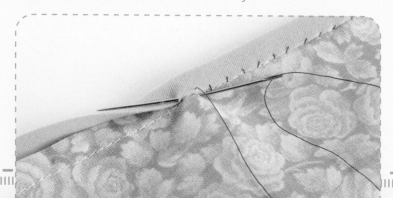

Creating mitred corners

1 Sew along the crease line as usual (see page 15), but stop ¼in (5mm) from the end of your work and reverse a couple of stitches.

2 Pinch the corner of the tape, matching up the raw edges with the second side of fabric.

3 Start sewing at the edge of the fabric, again along the crease line.

4 Fold the tape over and you'll see a neat fold in the corner.

5 When you've finished sewing the bias tape to the front, pin the corner, then hand sew on the back.

Fitting a magnetic clasp

These simple clasps don't usually come with instructions, so here's how to fit them. I'd recommend placing a scrap of fabric behind the clasp, on the wrong side of your fabric, to stabilise the fabric and help to stop the clasps pulling. If you're fitting to a bag with a flap, the narrower side of the clasp will go on the flap and the wider section on the bag.

1 Mark the position of the clasp with an erasable ink pen – take the back of the clasp and draw through the two long holes.

2 Use your quick-unpick or a small pair of sharp scissors to make a small incision at each line. It's better to make the cuts too small so they can be made bigger – if you cut them too big you may ruin your project.

3 Push the prongs of the clasp through the holes, through a scrap of fabric and through the back of the clasp.

4 Open out the prongs on the back of the fabric. It doesn't really matter whether you open them outwards or close them inwards – personally I find them easier to open outwards. Repeat for the other half of the clasp.

Adding a vintage touch

To add that authentic vintage touch to your projects, choose your colours carefully. Imagine tones of colour that would have been bold a hundred years ago, but have faded over time to create muted soft pastels. Florals, linen and lace would have been popular choices in previous eras, and aren't difficult to find nowadays. I bought my doilies (right) from an auction site online – I love the thought of someone carefully crocheting or tatting these beautiful items long ago.

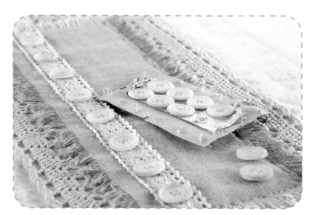

These shell buttons I inherited from my Mum – as a dressmaker she collected all manner of notions!

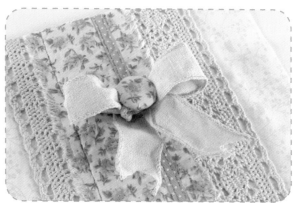

If you can't find a button to match, it's simple to cover your own with fabric of your choice.

I really enjoy free-motion embroidery and I think it gives a unique, home-made feel to your projects. You'll need a free-motion or darning foot for your sewing machine and you'll need to drop the feed dogs (although some machines have a plate that covers the feed dogs instead). Move the fabric under the needle to doodle with thread!

Try sewing ribbon over a strip of lace to create bespoke trimmings.

Pillow Cover

This simple envelope-style pillow cover has a nostalgic feel with its vintage doily, lace, ribbon and buttons. Although it looks like a buttoned cover, the buttons are actually just for decoration, so the faint-hearted amongst you don't need to worry about making buttonholes! You may prefer not to cut the doily if it's an antique, so I've wrapped this one around the fabric instead of cutting it. The pillow cover can be adapted to any size – simply add more buttons and lace if you wish!

Finished size

15 x 11in (38 x 28cm)

What you need

One piece of fabric measuring 15 x 11in (38 x 28cm)

One piece of fabric measuring 24 x 11in (61 x 28cm)

One piece of fabric measuring 16 x 11in (40.5 x 28cm)

Six covered buttons

One 12in (30.5cm) crocheted doily

One piece of floral fabric measuring 4 x 11in (10 x 28cm), frayed along the two long sides

One piece of craft lace measuring 6 x 11in (15.25 x 28cm)

One piece of 1in (2.5cm) wide lace, 11in (28cm) long

18in (45.75cm) of 1½in (4cm) wide hessian/burlap ribbon to make the bow

One piece of ½in (1cm) wide spot ribbon, 11in (28cm) long

15 x 11in (38 x 28cm) pillow pad

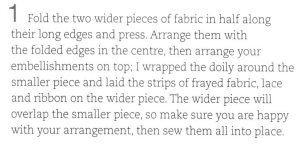

1 Fold the two wider pieces of fabric in half along their long edges and press. Arrange them with the folded edges in the centre, then arrange your embellishments on top; I wrapped the doily around the smaller piece and laid the strips of frayed fabric, lace and ribbon on the wider piece. The wider piece will overlap the smaller piece, so make sure you are happy with your arrangement, then sew them all into place.

2 Space five of the buttons evenly along the folded edge of the wider cover piece and hand sew in place. Make up and add the bow to the cover, with the remaining button in the centre.

3 Lay the buttoned section right sides together with the back piece of the pillow cover. Place the doily side over the top, with the raw edges together. Pin, then sew all the way round. Snip off the corners.

4 Remove the pins and turn right side out. To protect the lace and buttons, instead of pressing, give a light steam with your iron.

Tip
Make up a few pillows in different sizes – keep the tones of the colours uniform but vary the positioning of the buttons and bows.

Posy Cone

This simple cone is a perfect place to display a bunch of dried flowers or as simple storage for bobbins and threads. Hessian/burlap is a wonderfully earthy, organic-looking fabric that lends itself to a little ribbon and lace.

Finished size

5½ x 7½in (14 x 19cm)

What you need

10 x 17in (25.5 x 43cm) hessian/burlap

10 x 17in (25.5 x 43cm) natural cotton lining fabric

18in (45.75cm) of ½in (1cm) wide ribbon

18in (45.75cm) of ½in (1cm) wide lace

Tweezers (optional)

Button

Template, see page 95

Tip

Why not enlarge the cone to make a display of different sized posies!

1 Measure 3in (7.5cm) from the top of your hessian/burlap and gently pull out, one strand at a time, eight strands of thread (tweezers may help here). Thread the lace onto a large-eyed needle and weave through the hessian/burlap, going over and under four strands at a time.

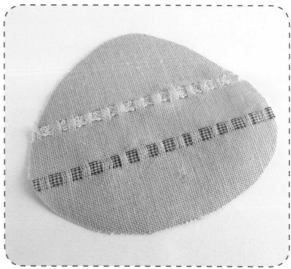

2 Measure about 1½in (4cm) below the lace and repeat, this time using ribbon to weave.

3 Cut one piece of your cone shape from hessian/burlap and one from cotton, using your template.

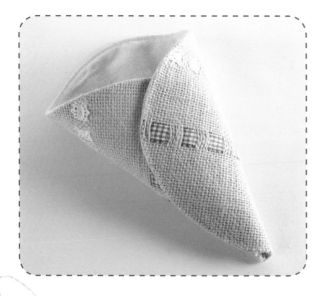

4 Sew the hessian/burlap right sides together with the cotton, leaving a turning gap of about 3in (7.5cm) in one side. Turn right side out and press, then top-stitch around the edge. Twist the fabric into a cone shape and pin, then hand sew around the curve to secure. Remove the pins.

5 Make a bow from the remaining ribbon. Add 4in (10cm) of lace folded in half to the back and sew to the front of the cone.

6 Sew the button to the centre top of the back of the cone, then make a tie from string pulled from a spare piece of hessian/burlap. Pop in your posy and hang!

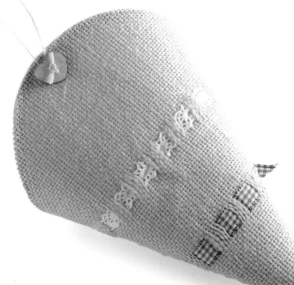

Jar Wraps

Make use of old jars by dressing them up in these simple wraps, decorated with flowers, buttons and bows!

Finished size

Large: 11 x 3½in (28 x 9cm)
Small: 11 x 2½in (28 x 6.5cm)

What you need

Clean jam jars

Strips of hessian/burlap long enough to wrap around the jars

1 x 10in (2.5 x 25.5cm) strip of hessian/burlap for the flower, frayed along one long edge

Button for the centre of the flower

8in (20.5cm) of ribbon to make a bow

Ribbon and lace long enough to wrap around the jars

1 Cut the hessian/burlap strips to the height of the jars, and long enough to wrap around them. As with the Posy Cone (see page 20), weave ribbon and lace through one of the strips, as shown. Fray the long edges of both a little.

2 To make up the flower, take a hand running stitch along one long edge and pull to gather.

3 Sew the button on the centre, then sew the flower to the plain hessian/burlap strip. Wrap this around the jar and secure with a spot of fabric glue. Repeat with the second jar, but add a bow instead of a flower.

Tray Mat

This pretty tray mat is perfect for serving up tea and sandwiches at an afternoon tea party, or you could make one for use in the bathroom or dressing room to store soaps and cosmetics.

Finished size

Made to measure

What you need

½yd (45.75cm) of fabric

Enough insulated wadding/batting to cover the base of your tray

Erasable ink pen

24in (61cm) ruler

48in (122cm) of ¼in (5mm) wide ribbon

Repositionable spray fabric adhesive

1 Measure the base of your tray and cut a piece of insulated wadding/batting to this size. Mine measures 13½ x 11in (34.5 x 28cm).

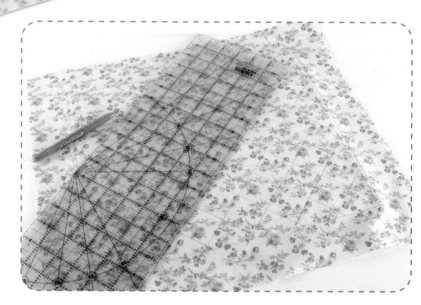

2 Measure the sides of your tray; add this to the size of the base and cut two pieces of fabric to this size plus ½in (1cm) for a seam allowance. The sides of my tray measure 2in (5cm) so my fabric pieces each measure 18 x 15½in (45.75 x 39.5cm).

3 Spray one side of the wadding/batting with adhesive and place centrally on the wrong side of the top piece of fabric. Draw around the edge of the wadding/batting on the right side of the fabric with your erasable ink pen. Draw a diagonal grid, with the lines 1½in (4cm) apart, to fill this rectangle.

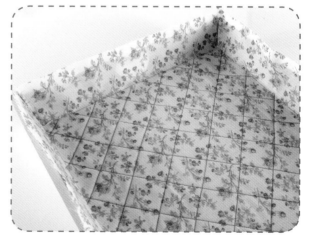

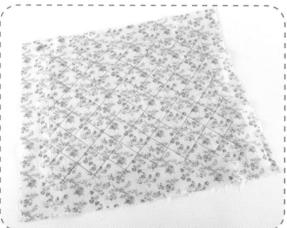

4 Sew across each diagonal line to quilt.

5 Place the mat inside the tray, and crease the corners of the fabric into the corners of the tray. Cut into the corners along the crease marks to remove a triangle of fabric from each corner.

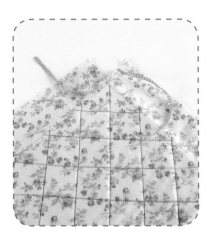

6 Tack/baste a piece of ribbon facing inwards to the right sides of these cut-out triangles, ½in (1cm) from the top.

7 Sew the two pieces of fabric right sides together, leaving a turning gap of about 4in (10cm) in one side. Don't yet cut the corners from the second piece of fabric.

8 As you sew around the corners, make a couple of stitches straight across the point – this will help the seam to sit flat when turned.

9 Now cut out the corners from the second piece of fabric. Turn right side out and press. Sew around the edge of the wadding/ batting through both layers of fabric. Top-stitch all the way around the edge.

10 Place the mat in your tray and tie the corners. Time for tea!

Bunting

Decorate your home inside and out with this easy embellished bunting! It's a great way of using left-over beads, buttons and flowers; pop a little lavender inside for a beautifully fragranced room!

Finished size

Each pennant: 4¼ x 8½in (11 x 21.5cm)

What you need

To make sixteen pennants:
¼yd (22.75cm) checked fabric
¼yd (22.75cm) spotted fabric
96in (244cm) of lace for hanging
18in (45.75cm) string of beads
18in (45.75cm) spot ribbon
18in (45.75cm) plain ribbon
Three posies of small silk flowers
Other embellishments

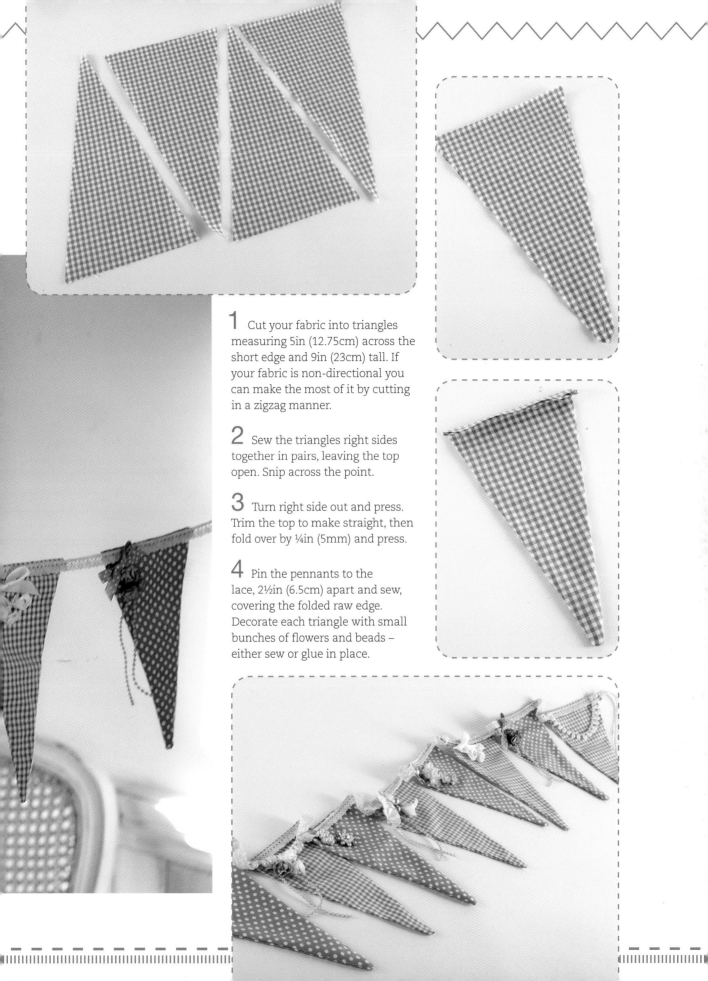

1 Cut your fabric into triangles measuring 5in (12.75cm) across the short edge and 9in (23cm) tall. If your fabric is non-directional you can make the most of it by cutting in a zigzag manner.

2 Sew the triangles right sides together in pairs, leaving the top open. Snip across the point.

3 Turn right side out and press. Trim the top to make straight, then fold over by ¼in (5mm) and press.

4 Pin the pennants to the lace, 2½in (6.5cm) apart and sew, covering the folded raw edge. Decorate each triangle with small bunches of flowers and beads – either sew or glue in place.

Bucket Bag

This pretty bag would be useful to store sewing items for the nursery or for cosmetics!

Finished size

7 x 11in (17.75 x 28cm)

What you need

Two circles of fabric, one outer and one lining, each measuring 8in (20.5cm) across

Two rectangles of fabric, one outer and one lining, each measuring 25 x 7in (63.5 x 17.75cm)

One circle of foam stabiliser measuring 7in (17.75cm) across

One length of foam stabiliser measuring 24 x 6in (61 x 15.25cm)

One rectangle of lining fabric for the drawstring section measuring 25 x 10in (63.5 x 25.5cm)

30in (76cm) of cord

Two lengths of 25in (63.5cm) long lace, or ribbon if you prefer, to decorate

For the handle, one strip of foam stabiliser measuring ½ x 13in (1 x 33cm)

One strip of fabric measuring 2 x 14in (5 x 35.5cm)

Two buttons

Repositionable spray fabric adhesive

Bodkin or safety pin

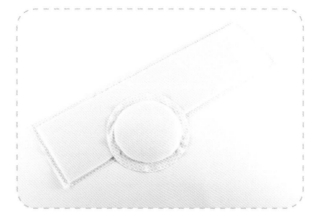

1 Fuse the stabiliser centrally to the wrong sides of the outer circle and side fabric pieces.

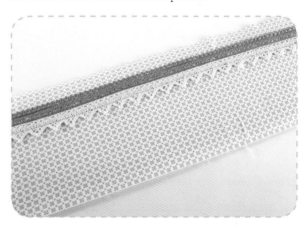

2 Decorate the outer panel with lace, ribbon or whatever you choose.

3 Hem the two short edges of the drawstring fabric by folding the fabric over ¼in (5mm), then ¼in (5mm) again and stitching.

4 Fold in half lengthways and press. Sew ½in (1cm) down from the fold to make a channel for the drawstring.

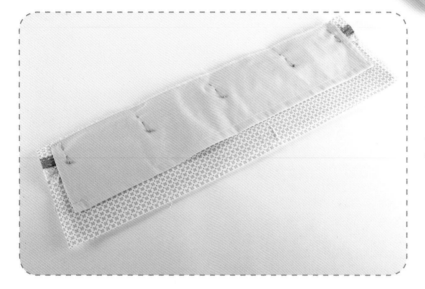

5 Edge stitch along the hemmed sides, avoiding the channel. Sew this panel centrally to the top of the outer section.

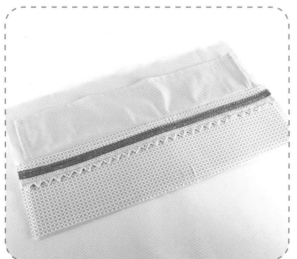

6 Sew the lining to the opposite side, sandwiching the drawstring section in the centre.

7 Fold the whole panel right sides together and sew along the side. Leave a gap in the lining for turning.

8 Pin then sew the two circular bases in place. Turn the right way out, and sew the gap closed. Push the lining inside the bag and press.

9 To make the handle, spray the strip of foam stabiliser with repositionable adhesive, and wrap the fabric around it, tucking in all raw edges. Sew straight down the centre.

10 Use a bodkin or safety pin to thread the cord through the channel.

11 Hand sew the handle to each side of the top of the bag with strong thread, then add a button to hide your stitches.

Tissuebox Cover

Cover a tissuebox with fabric to match your home decor. Decorate with ribbons and flowers for a pretty handmade gift!

Finished size

9 x 3 x 4½in (23 x 7.5 x 11.5cm)

What you need

For a box measuring 9 x 3 x 4½in (23 x 7.5 x 11.5cm):

One piece of outer fabric measuring 16½ x 21in (42 x 53.5cm)

One piece of lining measuring 16½ x 21in (42 x 53.5cm)

One piece of wadding/batting measuring 16½ x 21in (42 x 53.5cm)

44in (112cm) of ½in (1cm) wide ribbon

Sprig of paper flowers

6in (15.25cm) bead trim

Repositionable spray fabric adhesive

1 Cut a 6in (15.25cm) square from each corner of the outer fabric, lining and wadding/batting. Fuse the wadding/batting to the wrong side of the outer fabric with spray adhesive.

2 Measure and mark 3in (7.5cm) from the top of each corner on both the outer and lining pieces.

3 Taking the outer fabric piece, sew each corner right sides together up to these marks, then turn the piece right side out.

4 Repeat step 3 with the lining fabric, but on one corner leave a turning gap of 2in (5cm).

5 Cut four lengths of 10in (25.5cm) long ribbon, tack/baste them to the long top sides, 1in (2.5cm) in from the corners.

6 Drop the outer piece (which is the right way out) inside the lining (which is still inside out) so that the right sides are touching. Sew around the top. You'll find it easier to sew across the top of the four pieces first, then sew along the 'v' shapes in the corners afterwards.

7 Snip across the corners and carefully turn right side out. This will be a bit of a squeeze but persevere – it will work! Press, then top-stitch around the edge.

8 Use your remaining ribbon to knot around the sprig of flowers and bead trim.

9 Hand sew the posy to the front of the box cover, pop in your tissues and tie up the bows. Trim away a little of the ribbon if necessary.

Notebook Cover

Whether you're jotting down favourite recipes or making notes in a meeting, do it in style with this beautifully bound book!

Tip
This is a great way to use up any odd buttons and beads, and would make a beautiful cover for a family photo album.

Finished size

9½ x 13½in (24 x 34.25cm)

What you need

To cover an 8¼ x 11¾in (210 x 297mm/A4) notebook you will need:

Two pieces of plain fabric measuring 6in (15.25cm) wider and 1in (2.5cm) taller than your open book: I've used linen but calico would make an affordable alternative

One piece of wadding/batting measuring the same

Seven vintage buttons

Twelve pearl beads

Four paper flowers

18in (45.75cm) piece of 1in (2.5cm) wide lace

30in (76cm) piece of ½in (1cm) wide ribbon

A piece of linen or calico measuring 3 x 9in (7.5 x 23cm), frayed around the edge

A piece of contrasting fabric measuring 4 x 10in (10 x 25.5cm), frayed around the edge

Erasable ink pen

Repositionable spray fabric adhesive

1 Stick the wadding/batting to the wrong side of the outer fabric with adhesive. Fold the outer fabric around your notebook and mark the front of the book – the area you're going to decorate – with erasable pen. Place your strips of frayed fabric in the centre of the marked area and sew, then position a strip of ribbon over a piece of lace and sew next to the frayed pieces.

2 Make a bow from the remaining lace and a piece of ribbon and hand sew to the book cover. Sew the buttons evenly over the frayed fabric – I took the thread around the outside of the buttons to form a cross shape. Hand sew on the scattering of pearl beads and paper flowers. If your flowers are quite large, this may be easier to do when the cover is finished.

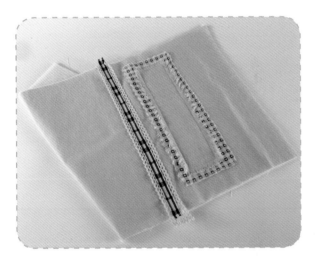

3 Tack/baste the remaining ribbon to the centre front of the cover, facing inwards. Trim to about 2in (5cm) longer than the cover. This will make the bookmark. Place the cover and lining fabrics right sides together, and sew all the way around, leaving a turning gap in one side and being careful to keep the ribbon out of the way of your stitch line! Snip off the corners, turn right side out and press. Fold the ends of the cover inwards to fit around your book. Top-stitch the two long edges.

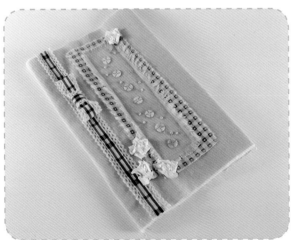

4 Slip your book inside!

Letter Holder

A stylish wall hanging decorated with bows and fabric flowers is the perfect place to keep postcards, letters and notelets. This letter holder can be made in any fabric to match your home decor – use it in your kitchen to keep favourite recipes to hand, or in your sewing room to store small scissors and notions.

Finished size

13½ x 27½in (34.25 x 70cm)

What you need

Two pieces of fabric measuring 14 x 23in (35.5 x 58.5cm): I've used a plain grey for the front and a patterned fabric on the back

One strip of contrasting fabric measuring 4½ x 21in (11.5 x 53.5cm), frayed around the edges

One strip of fabric measuring 2 x 19in (5 x 48.25cm), frayed around the edges

Six pieces of fabric for the hearts measuring 10in (25.5cm) square, in three designs

Four strips of torn fabric measuring 1 x 20in (2.5 x 51cm) for the flowers

Three pieces of black and two pieces of white 1in (2.5cm) wide ribbon, each 20in (51cm) long for the flowers

Two pieces of fabric to hang, each measuring 4 x 6in (10 x 15.25cm)

Three pieces of 6in (15.25cm) wide ribbon to make the bows, measuring 16in (40.5cm) in length

6in (15.25cm) length of bead trim

Hot glue gun or strong fabric glue

Rail for hanging

Marking pen

Template, see page 95

1 To make up the heart pockets, cut out six shapes from your template on page 95. Sew each pair right sides together, leaving a turning gap in one straight side of about 3in (7.5cm). Turn right side out and press. Measure 1½in (4cm) down from the top of the hearts, and top-stitch around the curved sides from one mark to the other.

2 To create the flowers, take a strip of fabric or ribbon and fold one end over to form a triangle. This doesn't have to be too neat.

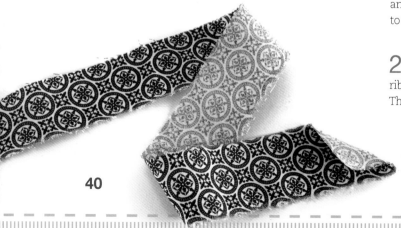

3 Begin to roll the end of the fabric; with every couple of turns, flip the fabric over. Add a spot of glue after every couple of twists to secure it.

4 Keep twisting and rolling until you reach the end of your fabric.

5 When your flower is completed, glue the end in place; you may have a point underneath the flower that needs to be trimmed. Glue across the bottom of the flower and leave to dry.

6 Place the two strips of frayed fabric along the right side centre of the front fabric piece and sew all the way around the edges.

7 Arrange the heart pockets along the frayed fabric, overlapping them slightly. Mark their position with a marking pen. Starting with the top heart, sew around the bottom of the pockets, joining the stitch line with the top-stitching you've already made.

8 Take the two strips of fabric for the hanging hoops, fold each in half lengthways, then in half again and press. Top-stitch along the folded edges.

9 Fold these in half, pin, then tack/baste, facing inwards, to the top of the backing fabric, 3in (7.5cm) in from each corner. Remove the pins.

10 Place the backing fabric on top, right sides together, and sew all the way round, leaving a turning gap of about 4in (10cm) in one side. Turn right side out and press. Top-stitch all the way round.

11 Glue three flowers to each pocket, with a bow underneath. Add a couple of strings of bead trim to the centre pocket.

Tip
You could sew the flowers on instead of gluing them on if you prefer, and if you'd like the fabric to feel a little firmer, add wadding/batting to the wrong side of the backing fabric.

Floral Wreath

This stylish wreath makes such a pretty decoration for your home, to hang on a door or over the bed; it would also make a beautiful wedding present!

1 Tear six strips of linen, approx. 1½in (4cm) wide, and make up six flowers using the same method as for the letter holder on page 42. Try using different widths of fabric to make smaller or larger sizes.

2 For the felt flowers, cut three 2in (5cm) circles, then cut these in half. Overlap five of these half circles in a row.

3 Sew a running stitch across the straight edge by hand.

4 Pull to gather, overlap the ends and stitch to secure in a circle.

5 Add a bead or button to the centre.

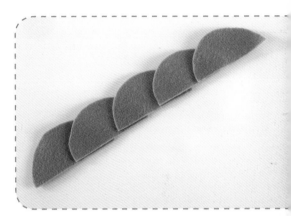

6 To make the lace flowers, sew a running stitch along one side of the lace strip...

7 ... pull to gather, then add a rustic-looking button or bead to the centre.

8 Make up around twelve flowers.

9 Tear the linen fabric into 2in (5cm) wide strips. Wrap around the wire wreath, securing with spots of hot glue here and there.

10 Make up a bow from a 15in (38cm) length of torn linen.

11 Wrap the twine and lace around the wreath, securing with hot glue. Wrap the cord, but this time leave a large loop for hanging. Now for the fun bit: arrange the flowers, bead trim, bows and buttons to one side of the hoop, and when you're happy with the arrangement, secure in place with hot glue.

Tip

Be careful when using a hot glue gun as the glue really does get very hot! To remove the fine hair-like strands of glue, give them a waft with a heat gun, if you have one, and they'll just disappear!

Dressing Table Mat

When I was a young girl, I remember seeing my auntie's hairbrush, comb and mirror set on her dressing table mat – I thought this was so stylish! This pretty mat has a modern twist with dragonfly appliqué and polka dot fabric, but still evokes the glamour of yesteryear!

Finished size

18 x 12in (45.75 x 30.5cm)

What you need

One rectangle of fabric for the top measuring 11 x 17in (28 x 43cm)

One rectangle of fabric for the base measuring 11 x 18in (28 x 45.75cm)

Wadding/batting measuring 11 x 17in (28 x 43cm)

A 12in (30.5cm) circle template

75in (190.5cm) of 1½in (4cm) wide lace

Erasable ink pen

Contrasting fabric for the appliqué pieces, approximately 10in (25.5cm) square

Fusible adhesive sheets

Template, see page 95

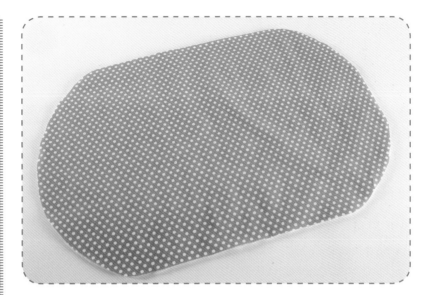

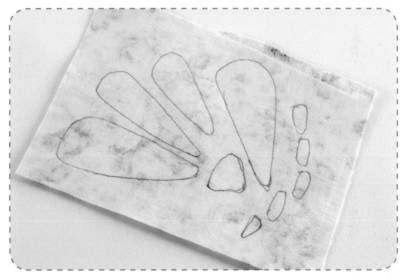

1 Cut the 18in (45.75cm) piece of fabric in half, then sew back together with a ½in (1cm) seam allowance. Press open the seam. Place the two pieces of fabric together, and using your circle template, draw then cut around each end of both to form the oval shape. Cut a piece of wadding/batting to this shape.

2 Fuse the adhesive sheet to the wrong side of your appliqué fabric, draw around the template on page 95, and cut out two dragonflies, so that you can overlap the wings.

3 Place the appliqué shapes in position on the front of your mat (the unstitched piece), take off the paper backing and iron in place.

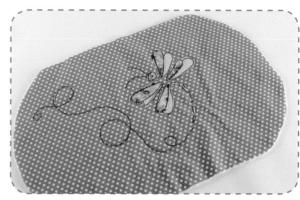

4 Using a thread colour that will be visible, free-motion embroider a few times around the edge of your dragonfly shapes.

5 Free hand draw a swirly line with your erasable ink pen and free-motion embroider over it.

6 Gather your length of lace with a running stitch along one long edge.

7 Pin it evenly around the edge of the mat, facing inwards and overlapping slightly when the two ends meet. Tack/baste in place.

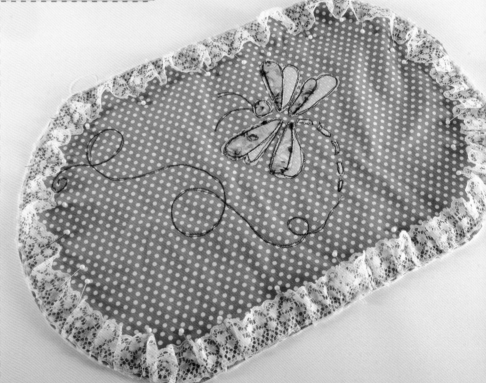

8 Remove the pins. Sew the front and back pieces of fabric right sides together, then take a quick unpick or small sharp scissors and unpick some of the stitches in the centre back seam.

9 Trim around the curves with pinking shears, then turn right side out and press. Hand sew the opening in the seam closed, then machine top-stitch around the mat.

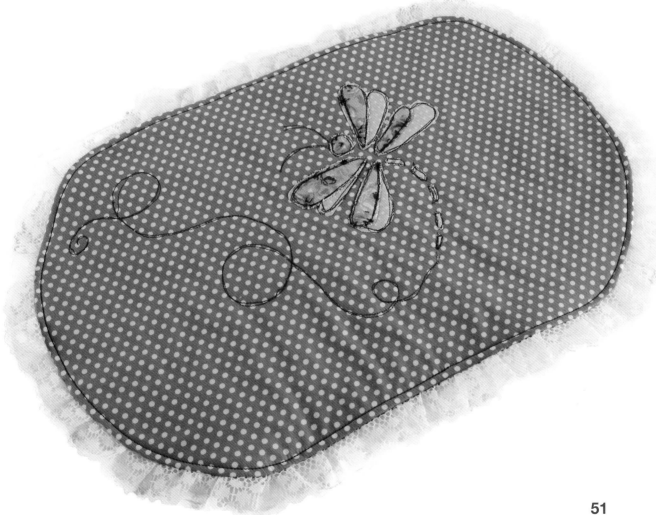

Glasses Case

This stylish pouch will store and protect your glasses or sunglasses. I made mine to match my dressing table cover, but use any colours you like!

Finished size

3¹⁄₃ x 6½in (8.5 x 16.5cm)

What you need

Two 4 x 10in (10 x 25.5cm) rectangles of fabric

Two 4 x 7in (10 x 17.75cm) rectangles of contrast fabric

10in (25.5cm) square of fusible wadding/batting

16in (40.5cm) of ¼in (5mm) wide ribbon

20in (51cm) of 1½in (4cm) wide lace

8in (20.5cm) of ½in (1cm) wide lace

4in (10cm) circle template

Marker pen

Elastic hair tie

Three buttons

1 Fuse the wadding/batting to the wrong sides of one long and one short fabric piece. Using your circle template, cut a curve around the top of each piece of fabric.

2 Hand sew a running stitch along the centre of the 1½in (4cm) wide lace and pull to gather an 8in (20.5cm) strip. Tack/baste, then machine sew this to the centre front piece of the case (the piece with wadding/batting attached).

3 Sew a length of ribbon over the gathered lace, then sew the buttons over the ribbon, the first one 3in (7.5cm) from the top (refer to step 4 for placing). Sew the two shorter pieces right sides together around the curved top edge.

4 Turn right side out and press. Top-stitch around the curved edge.

5 Place this piece right sides together with the unbacked larger piece, and sew along one straight side.

6 Tack/baste the elastic hair tie facing inwards to the right side centre top of the remaining large piece.

8 Make a bow from ribbon and lace and hand sew it to the front of the case. Fold over the flap and fasten.

7 Sew this piece right sides together with the first section – leave a turning gap in the same side you've already stitched of about 3in (7.5cm). Turn right side out and hand sew the opening closed. Turn again so that the hand-sewn seam is on the inside.

Birdhouse Peg Bag

The garden birds will be quite envious of this vintage-inspired clothes peg/pin bag! The birdhouse 'roof' is shaped by the curve of the coat hanger, so it can be made to fit any size hanger you like.

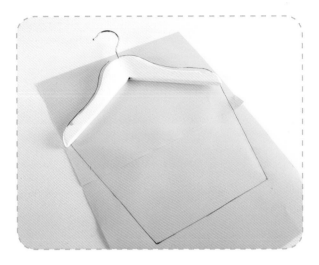

Finished size

12½ x 14in (31.75 x 35.5cm)

What you need

A child's coat hanger: mine measures 12in (30.5cm) across

15 x 30in (38 x 76.25cm) outer fabric

15 x 30in (38 x 76.25cm) lining fabric

15 x 30in (38 x 76.25cm) fusible wadding/batting

14 x 12in (35.5 x 30.5cm) plain fabric for the roof

7in (17.75cm) of 3in (7.5cm) wide lace

8in (20.5cm) of ¾in (2cm) wide gingham ribbon for the bow

8in (20.5cm) of 1in (2.5cm) wide lace for the bow

16in (40.5cm) of ¾in (2cm) wide lace for the roof trim

6in (15.25cm) of ½in (1cm) wide lace for the hanger bow

20in (51cm) of ¼in (5mm) wide ribbon to wrap around the hook

Card and marking tool to make a template

A 5in (12.75cm) circle template

Fabric glue

1 Place your coat hanger on the card and draw around the top curve. Measure and mark a line 14in (35.5cm) down from the top of the hanger, then two lines down the sides, tapered inwards so that the base measures 8in (20.5cm) across.

2 Cut out this template shape; fold the card in half to make sure it is symmetrical. Adding 1in (2.5cm) all the way round, cut two pieces of outer fabric, two pieces of lining and two pieces of wadding/batting. Fuse each wadding/batting piece to the wrong side of an outer piece.

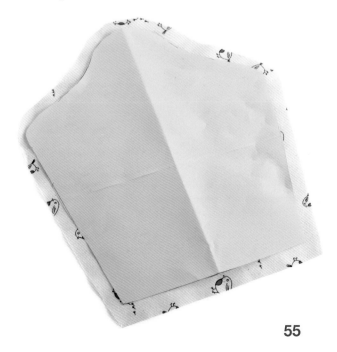

3 To make the roof shape, draw around the top of your outer fabric onto plain fabric, then draw another line to the same shape, 1¼in (3.25cm) below. Curve the ends. This roof shape should fit over your outer fabric as in the picture. Cut two roof pieces.

4 Sew the two roof pieces right sides together around the bottom side. Turn right side out and press. Place over the top of one outer piece and topstitch across the seam to attach.

5 Draw a circle using your 5in (12.75cm) template centrally on the back of one lining piece, 5in (12.75cm) from the top of the birdhouse.

6 Pin the lining to the outer piece with the roof, right sides together, and sew around the circle. Cut out the circle shape with an ⅛in (3mm) seam allowance.

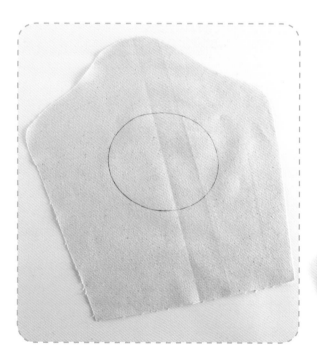

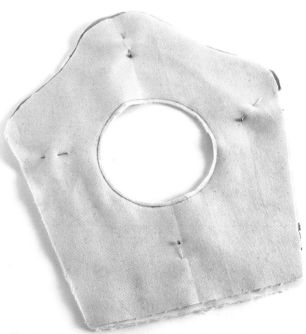

7 Remove the pins and snip into the curved seam. Push the lining through the hole and press. Topstitch around the edge of the hole, then sew the strip of lace trim just under the roof. Make up the bow from ribbon and lace and hand sew in place to one side of the hole.

8 Place the remaining outer fabric piece right sides together with the first and sew across the bottom edge.

9 The remaining lining side will go over the top – you will have one lining piece on top and one on the bottom of the sandwich. Sew around the top sides, leaving the bottom edge open, and leaving a ¼in (5mm) gap at the top of the roof to fit the hanger hook.

10 Turn right side out with the linings together and hand sew the opening closed, then turn again so that the lining is on the inside. Hand sew the large strip of lace behind the hole to help stop the pegs/pins from falling out. Wrap the 20in (51cm) length of ribbon around the hook of the hanger and glue the ends to secure. Thread the hook of the hanger through the gap in the roof and pull the house over the hanger. Add a lace bow to the base of the hook to finish.

Hanging Hearts

This is such a simple way to create a pretty decoration for any room in your home! Use your favourite fabrics, and embellish each heart with ribbons, lace, buttons and bows – get as creative as you like! The measurements are for one heart, which would make a beautiful decoration on its own, but three hearts hanging from a painted coat hanger really makes a statement. I painted my coat hanger with white emulsion paint, then sanded it slightly when dry to give it an aged look.

Finished size

Each heart 8 x 8in
(20.5 x 20.5cm)

What you need

Two squares of fabric measuring 10in (25.5cm)

Approximately 9oz (250g) toy filler

8 x 2in (20.5 x 5cm) strip of linen fabric, frayed along the long edges

8 x 1½in (20.5 x 4cm) strip of netting

8in (20.5cm) of ½in (1cm) lace

8in (20.5cm) of ¼in (5mm) wide ribbon

Three shell buttons

Fabric flowers

1½ x 15in (4 x 38cm) netting to make a bow

Hot glue gun or strong fabric glue

Wooden coat hanger, with three fabric flowers, 12in (30.5cm) lace and 12in (30.5cm) ribbon to decorate

20in (51cm) of ribbon or twine to hang

Template, see page 95

1 Cut one square of fabric in half, then sew back together with a ½in (1cm) seam allowance. Press the seam open. Place your heart template (see page 95) over the seam and cut out the shape, then cut another heart from the remaining square of fabric.

2 Arrange your buttons, frayed fabric, netting, lace and ribbon strips on the front of the unseamed heart.

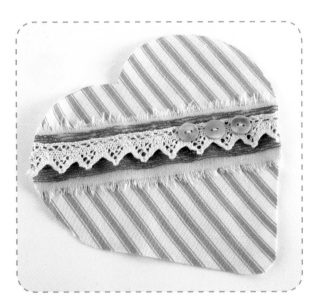

3 When you're happy with the arrangement, sew each piece in place, apart from any beads and bows that won't go under your machine foot – these will be glued or sewn on later.

4 Sew the two heart pieces right sides together with a small stitch on your machine – this will make a strong seam to withstand stuffing. When you come to sewing the 'v' shape at the top of the heart, sew a couple of stitches straight across the point – this will make it neater when turned. Trim the curves with pinking shears. Unpick around 7.5cm (3in) of stitches in the centre back seam.

5 Turn right side out and stuff tightly with toy filler. Hand sew the opening closed.

6 Add any bows, beads and flowers at this point: a hot glue gun will give the quickest adhesion. Hand sew a loop of ribbon to the centre top to hang – hide the stitches with a small bow or flower. If you're hanging from a coat hanger, wait until you have all three hearts so that you can arrange them at different lengths.

7 Experiment with different designs to your hearts: add a lace doily, make your own fabric flowers from page 42, or simply leave them plain!

8 Make a bow from ribbon and lace, glue this to the centre of the coat hanger, then add three flowers.

9 Sew three strips of ribbon or twine to the tops of the hearts, wrap the ribbon around the coat hanger and sew back on to the hearts. Pop a little glue behind the ribbon to hold them in place.

Tip
Why not add a little lavender or rose oil to the filling to give your room a beautiful aroma?

Shabby Chic Advent Calendar

Combining linen and lace evokes a nostalgic feel to this vintage-style calendar. It's really simple to make, and it's easy to personalise and embellish as much as you wish!

1 Fray the edges of your five linen strips. Lay the lace strips on top of the frayed linen pieces and sew together.

2 Iron the wadding/batting to the back of one of your large calico pieces. Pin the strips across the calico, starting 1½in (4cm) from the bottom and with a 1in (2.5cm) space in between each strip. Sew across the bottom of each strip, ½in (1cm) from the frayed edge. Remove the pins.

Finished size

18½ x 28in (47 x 71cm)

What you need

Two pieces of calico or natural cotton measuring 20 x 23in (51 x 58.5cm)

One piece of fusible wadding/batting measuring 20 x 23in (51 x 58.5cm)

Five strips of torn linen measuring 20 x 3½in (51 x 9cm): it needs to fray – a loosely woven fabric will fray more easily

Five strips of lace each measuring 20in (51cm) in length, any width up to 3in (7.5cm)

One piece of linen measuring 40 x 5in (101.75 x 12.75cm), frayed by about 1in (2.5cm) along one long edge

Two pieces of lace to hang, 8in (20.5cm) each in length

Two large buttons

I used seven buttons as decorations: add as few or as many as you like

16in (41cm) hessian/burlap ribbon to make two bows

6in (15.25cm) string tied around one bow

Approximately 30in (76cm) lace to make bows

Small bunches of paper flowers

6in (15.25cm) bead trim

Numbers 1–25: I've used stamps here

Erasable marking pen

Strong fabric glue

Rail to hang, up to 20in (51cm) in length: I used a coat hanger that I spraypainted white then sanded for an aged look

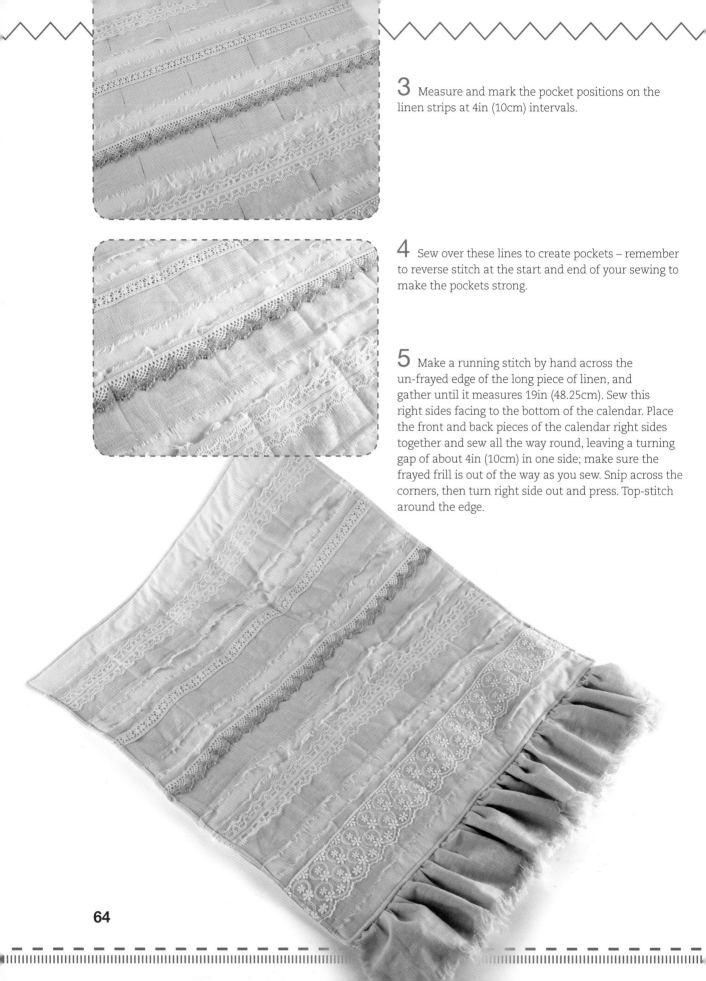

3 Measure and mark the pocket positions on the linen strips at 4in (10cm) intervals.

4 Sew over these lines to create pockets – remember to reverse stitch at the start and end of your sewing to make the pockets strong.

5 Make a running stitch by hand across the un-frayed edge of the long piece of linen, and gather until it measures 19in (48.25cm). Sew this right sides facing to the bottom of the calendar. Place the front and back pieces of the calendar right sides together and sew all the way round, leaving a turning gap of about 4in (10cm) in one side; make sure the frayed frill is out of the way as you sew. Snip across the corners, then turn right side out and press. Top-stitch around the edge.

6 Stamp your numbers onto fabric; I found a fabric with small hearts and stars on and stamped over the pattern.

7 Cut around the numbers to create squares measuring approximately 1in (2.5cm); fray the edges slightly. Glue a number to each pocket.

8 Now for the fun bit: add a bow to the bottom centre of the calendar, the bow at the top I tied with string. Add fabric flowers and beads as you wish! Make two loops of lace and sew to the top of the calendar, 5in (12.75cm) in from each corner. Cover your stitches with two large buttons.

9 Thread onto a rail and hang! If you're using a coat hanger, fold the lace loops over the hanger before sewing in place.

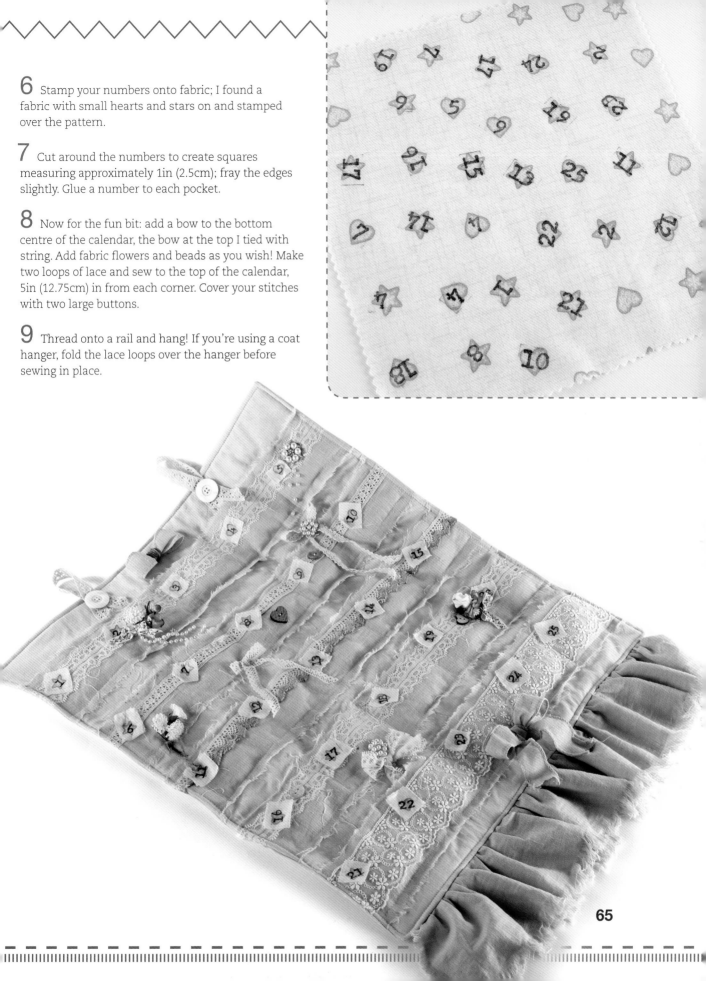

Doily Clutch

I designed this bag around a beautiful crocheted doily with pansies around the edge, as I thought it would look perfect on a bag flap.

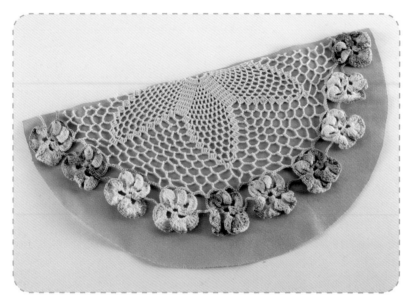

Finished size

13 x 9in (33 x 23cm)

What you need

A crocheted doily: mine measures 11in (28cm) across

Circle of plain fabric, 12in (30.5cm) across

Two 13 x 8in (33 x 20.5cm) rectangles of outer fabric

Two 13 x 8in (33 x 20.5cm) rectangles of lining fabric: I used the same fabric

Two 13 x 8in (33 x 20.5cm) pieces of fusible fleece

Magnetic clasp

3in (7.5cm) circle template

1 Cut the circle of plain fabric and the doily in half. Hand stitch the doily to one piece of fabric.

2 Mark the centre point of the remaining semi-circle of fabric by folding it in half and creasing. Apply the thin half of the magnetic clasp 1¼in (3cm) up from the curved edge.

3 Sew this piece right sides together with the doily side, leaving the straight side open. Clip into the curve, then turn right side out and press. Edge stitch around the curve.

Tip
Try auction websites and charity shops to find vintage doilies.

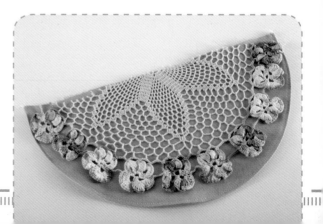

4 Fuse the fleece to the wrong sides of the outer fabric rectangles. Round off the bottom corners of all the rectangular pieces of fabric using your circle template. Place the flap over the top of one outer piece and mark where the second half of the magnetic clasp will fit.

5 Fit the clasp over this mark.

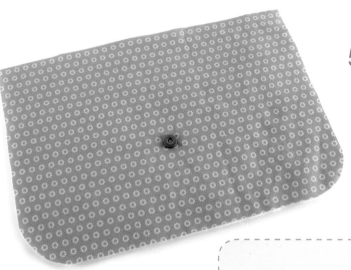

6 Sew the flap to the back piece of the bag, along the straight edge, right sides together.

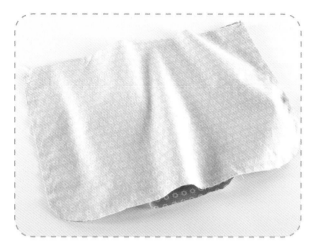

7 Sew the two outer sections of the bag right sides together, leaving the top open. Sew the lining pieces together in the same way, also leaving a gap in the bottom for turning.

8 Turn the lining section the right side out. Drop it inside the outer bag so that the right sides are together. Sew around the top, lining up the side seams. Turn the bag right side out through the gap in the lining, then sew the opening closed.

9 Push the lining inside the bag and press.

Shabby Chic Christmas Stocking

I'm sure this stylish stocking won't be put away after Christmas – fill it with silk flowers to make a beautiful year-round decoration! Embellish your stocking with anything you like: ribbons, lace, flowers, leaves and beads. You really can't add too much, but try to keep the colours neutral to create the vintage look.

Finished size

About 7 x 18in (17.75 x 45.75cm)

What you need

A man's sock, card and pen to make a template

30 x 18in (76 x 45.75cm) fabric: I used linen

30 x 18in (76 x 45.75cm) lining fabric

30 x 18in (76 x 45.75cm) fusible wadding/batting

30 x 4in (76 x 10cm) strip of fabric, frayed by 1in (2.5cm) along one long side

12in (30.5cm) ribbon to hang

Six strips of lace in different widths, 10in (25.5cm) each in length

20in (51cm) bead trim

24in (61cm) ribbon and 24in (61cm) lace to decorate the back of the stocking

24in (61cm) ribbon and 24in (61cm) lace to make bows

Handful of buttons and seed beads

Three 8 x 5in (20.5 x 12.75cm) pieces of hessian/burlap to make the flowers

Three pearl beads

Hot glue gun

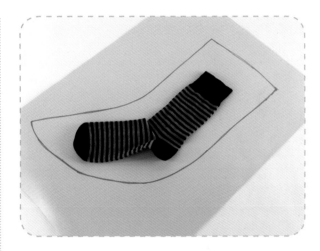

1 Press your sock flat. Place it on top of the card and draw around it, adding 2in (5cm) all around and extend the top so that the stocking measures about 18in (45.75cm). Draw a pointed toe.

2 Cut out the template. Fold your outer and lining fabrics in half, wrong sides facing, and use the template to cut two pieces from each; also cut two pieces from wadding/batting. Fuse the wadding/batting pieces to the wrong side of the outer pieces.

3 To make up the flowers, pull away 2in (5cm) of the horizontal strands from the centre of your hessian/burlap pieces.

4 Trim the sides of the strips to measure ¼in (5mm). You'll find this easier than fraying an exact sized piece, as sometimes too many strands come away and your fabric becomes too small.

5 Fold a piece in half lengthways. Roll it up, adding a few spots of hot glue as you go. When each flower strip is completely rolled and glued, squash the centre to open out the 'petals' and add a pearl bead.

6 Arrange your strips of lace, bows, buttons, flowers and trim over your stocking front.

7 When you're happy with the arrangement, sew the strips in place. Hand sew the buttons and seed beads but don't sew them too close to the edge of the stocking – you want to avoid the seam allowance.

8 Sew the two outer pieces right sides together, leaving the top edge open. Turn right side out. Fold a 24in (61cm) piece of ribbon and lace in half and tack/baste to the top of the centre back seam. Make a loop from the hanging ribbon and tack/baste the raw ends over the top of the ribbon and lace strips.

9 Take the frayed strip of fabric and sew the short ends together to form a loop. Hand sew a running stitch along the un-frayed side and gather the loop until it measures 20in (51cm).

10 Push the stocking into the frayed fabric loop with the right sides together and sew, with the seam of the loop to the back of the stocking.

11 Sew the lining pieces right sides together leaving the top edge open and with a turning gap of about 4in (10cm) in the side seam. Put the outer fabric inside the lining so that the right sides are together and sew around the top. Turn right side out through the gap and sew the opening closed.

12 Push the lining inside the stocking and press. Add your flowers, bead trim, bows and any other embellishments using your hot glue gun.

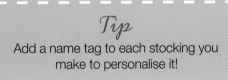

Tip
Add a name tag to each stocking you make to personalise it!

Little Cottages

Pretty and practical, these cute cottages can help to keep your home free from draughts or would make a delightful window decoration.

Finished size

25 x 8in (63.5 x 20.5cm)

What you need

18 x 8in (45.75 x 20.5cm) plain light fabric

18 x 8in (45.75 x 20.5cm) lightly patterned fabric

36 x 8in (91.5 x 20.5cm) backing fabric

Small pieces of coordinating fabrics to decorate: a charm pack is perfect

Four buttons for door handles

Sprig of fabric flowers

6in (15.25cm) of ribbon to make a bow

16in (40.5cm) of ½in (1cm) wide lace

16in (40.5cm) of 1in (2.5cm) wide lace

9oz (250g) toy filler

Erasable ink pen and ruler

Free-motion embroidery foot for your machine (or simply use a straight stitch on your machine if you wish, or hand sew)

Fabric glue or spray adhesive (optional)

Weights such as pebbles or small bags of rice (optional)

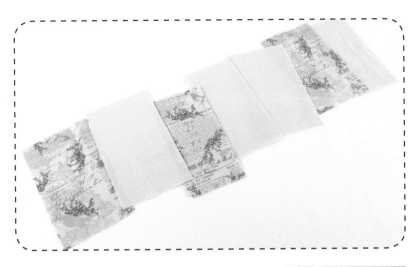

1 Cut seven rectangles of fabric. From plain fabric, cut two rectangles measuring 5 x 8in (12.75 x 20.5cm) and two measuring 4 x 8in (10 x 20.5cm). Cut two from patterned fabric measuring 5 x 8in (13 x 20.5cm) and one measuring 4 x 8in (10 x 20.5cm).

2 Measure and mark a line 3in (7.5cm) from the top of each rectangle, then mark from the centre of this line to the top.

3 Cut from the ends of the horizontal lines to different points on the vertical lines to create triangular roofs of differing heights.

4 Now to get decorating! Try to make every cottage different – add square and round windows, arched doors, lace eaves and curtain pelmets. Draw scalloped lines over a roof to embroider, and brickwork on another. Fray strips of fabric and lay them over each other on another roof. At this stage don't add anything that you can't sew over, such as buttons.

5 When you're happy with the arrangement, free-motion embroider around each piece of appliqué. You may find it useful to spray a little repositionable adhesive to the back of each piece to hold them in place while you sew.

6 Sew the cottages together side by side to make the row. Press.

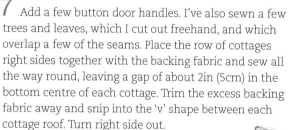

7 Add a few button door handles. I've also sewn a few trees and leaves, which I cut out freehand, and which overlap a few of the seams. Place the row of cottages right sides together with the backing fabric and sew all the way round, leaving a gap of about 2in (5cm) in the bottom centre of each cottage. Trim the excess backing fabric away and snip into the 'v' shape between each cottage roof. Turn right side out.

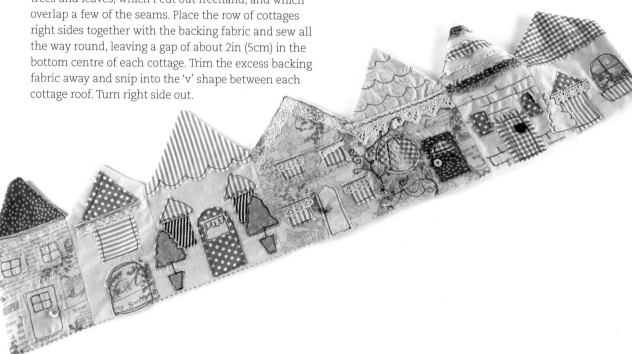

8 Top-stitch along the seam in between each cottage, forming seven pockets. Stuff each pocket with toy filler.

9 If you're using weights, pop these inside now, before hand sewing the openings closed. Tie a bow around a few of the fabric flowers and sew or glue to one of the end cottages; glue a couple more flowers to the cottage at the other end of the row.

Tip

Make up a few cottages individually and add a ribbon loop to the top to make Christmas decorations or lavender bags.

Tea Cosy

Keep your brew warmer for longer in this simple but stylish cosy! I've used insulated wadding/batting to help keep in the heat. As the cosy is made to measure, you can make it fit any pot you like.

Finished size

9 x 6in (23 x 15.25cm)

What you need

For a round 800ml (27 fl oz) tea pot:
9 x 35in (23 x 89cm) outer fabric
9 x 35in (23 x 89cm) lining
22 x 5in (56 x 12.75cm) insulated wadding/batting
15in (38cm) of 1in (2.5cm) wide bias binding
32in (81.25cm) of ¼in (5mm) wide ribbon
Erasable ink pen
Ruler
Hand sewing needle and strong thread
Quick unpick
Safety pin or bodkin

1 Measure the circular base of your tea pot – mine is 3in (7.5cm) across. Cut out circles from your outer fabric, your lining fabric and the wadding/batting that all measure 1in (2.5cm) larger than the tea pot base – so mine are 4in (10cm) across.

2 Place the two fabric circles wrong sides together with the wadding/batting sandwiched in between. Top-stitch close to the edge to hold the layers together. Mark the centre of each side of the circle.

3 Measure the height of your tea pot – mine is 6in (15.25cm). Add 1in (2.5cm) to this measurement. Cut two pieces of outer fabric and two pieces of lining to this length, the width is four times the measurement of the circle. So my pieces each measure 16 x 7in (40.5 x 17.75cm) Cut two pieces of wadding/batting to the same width (16in/40.5cm), but 2¼in (5.75cm) shorter in length (my wadding/batting measures 16 x 4¾in/40.5 x 12cm). Place the wadding/batting pieces onto the wrong side of the outer fabric pieces, ¼in (5mm) up from the bottom edge.

4 Sew a lining piece to an outer piece right sides together, leaving the bottom edge open. Snip across the corners, turn right side out and press. Tack/baste closely along the bottom edge. Draw two lines across each piece, 1½in (4cm) and 2in (5cm) from the top. Stitch along these lines. Use your quick unpick to undo the stitches in the side seams in between the sewn lines – this will create a channel for your ribbon tie. Repeat for the other two fabric pieces.

5 Take your needle and strong thread and make a running stitch across the bottom of each piece.

6 Gather the running stitch so that the length of the fabric is the same as the distance between the halfway marks on the circular base. Loosely over-edge stitch right sides together to the base.

7 Repeat with the second side.

8 Sew the bias tape around the raw edge; turn under the end of the tape and machine sew from the gathered side, overlapping the tape when the ends meet. Take it slowly as you sew, making sure the gathers are flat and the raw edges of the base and sides meet. Fold the tape over the raw edge and hand sew with a slip stitch.

9 Thread the ribbon onto your safety pin or bodkin and take this through both of the sewn channels. Pull each end to gather evenly, pop your tea pot inside and tie the ribbon into a bow.

Cake Frill

The frill can be adapted to any size of cake, square or round – simply measure the circumference of the cake to find the width of your fabric; the depth of the cake minus 1in (2.5cm) is the depth of the fabric.

Finished size

To fit a cake 8in (20.5cm) in diameter and 5in (12.75cm) deep

What you need

24 x 4in (61 x 10cm) gingham fabric

24 x 4in (61 x 10cm) laminated cotton (food-safe laminated fabrics are available)

45in (114.5cm) of 1in (2.5cm) wide ribbon

48in (122cm) of 1in (2.5cm) wide broderie anglaise trim

6in (15.25cm) squares of red stripe, green spot, blue spot and yellow fabrics for the appliqué

12 x 12in (30.5 x 30.5cm) fusible adhesive sheet

24 x 4in (61 x 10cm) tear-away stabiliser (optional)

Seven small beads

Erasable ink pen

Cupcake template, page 95

1 Measure and mark 2in (5cm) in from each end of the gingham fabric strip. Place the ribbon centrally over the top, and sew all the way around the inside edge of the ribbon to form a box shape with your stitches, in between the marks you've made.

2 Cut the broderie anglaise trim in half, and sew each piece facing inwards to a long edge of the gingham piece.

3 Iron your fusible adhesive to the wrong side of the 6in (15.25cm) fabric squares. Trace around the cupcake template on page 95 onto the paper backing of your fusible sheets to create seven cupcakes. Cut them out, remove the paper backing and iron them centrally over the ribbon in the middle of the gingham fabric. Draw swirly lines over the icing and pleats over the cups with your erasable ink pen.

4 Place the tear-away stabiliser behind the cupcakes and free-motion embroider around each cupcake and over your drawn lines.

5 With the trimmings and ribbon facing inwards, place the laminated backing and the gingham piece right sides together. Turn back the ends of the broderie anglaise trim so you don't sew them into the ends of the frill. Sew all the way round, leaving a turning gap of about 3in (7.5cm) in one long side. Snip off the corners, turn right side out and top-stitch all the way round. Hand sew a small bead to the top of each cake.

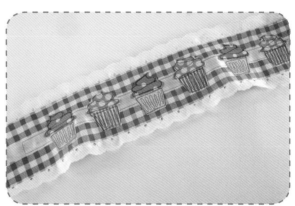

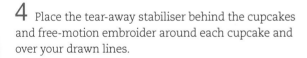

Tip
Instead of using free-motion embroidery, you could hand sew the appliqué with a blanket stitch.

Repair Kit

Every home should have needles, thread, scissors and buttons for those times when a quick repair is needed. This would make a perfect gift for someone who's leaving home for the first time, or as a housewarming present. Crazy patchwork is a really simple way of creating a distinctive look, and a great way to use up scraps of fabric.

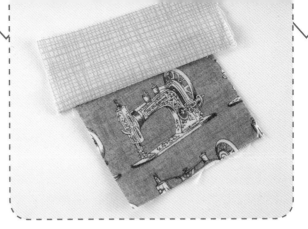

Finished size

9 x 11in (23 x 28cm)

What you need

11 x 12in (28 x 30.5cm) lining fabric

Ten 12in (30.5cm) strips of 1½in (4cm) wide fabric in three prints, to be cut to size

11 x 12in (28 x 30.5cm) wadding/batting

3in (7.5cm) square of fabric: I've cut a sewing machine from the print of my fabric

Elastic hair tie

Button

12in (30.5cm) piece of ½in (1cm) wide elastic

6in (15.25cm) ribbon

10 x 3in (25.5 x 7.5cm) felt

45in (114.5cm) of ¾in (2cm) wide bias binding

Repair kit items, for example: needles, pins, safety pins, four spools of thread, selection of buttons in different sizes, 4in (10cm) scissors

Erasable ink pen

Ruler

1 Take the square of fabric and place a 3in (7.5cm) strip of fabric right sides together at an angle to the top edge and sew. Turn the fabric strip over and press with your fingers.

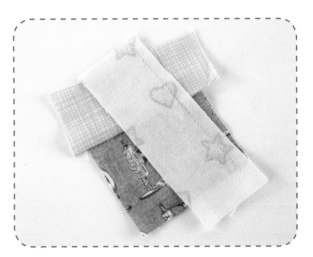

2 Place a second strip right sides together at a slight angle to the right-hand side of the square and sew. Each strip you now add should be long enough to cover the previous, so the strips will get longer each time.

3 Keep adding the strips in a clockwise direction, pressing each piece as you go.

4 As the shape started as a square and we need an oblong shape, add a strip of fabric to the top and bottom but not the sides, until you have a piece of patchwork measuring 9 x 11in (23 x 28cm). Trim to this size. Place over the wadding/batting and trim this to the same size. Hand sew a few lines of running stitch to add a little texture and to secure the fabric to the wadding/batting.

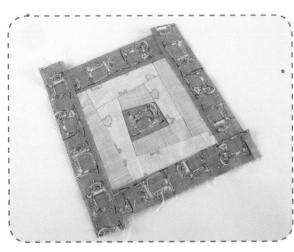

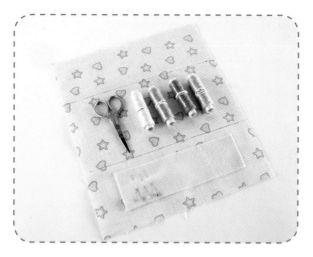

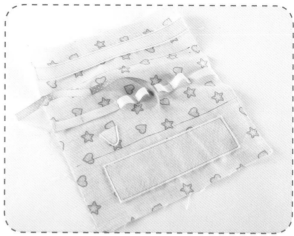

5 Cut your lining fabric to the same size. Measure and mark a line 3in (7.5cm) down from the top and another 3½in (9cm) up from the bottom – these will be the fold lines. Cut a strip of felt measuring 6½ x 2in (16.5 x 5cm) – this will hold your pins. Arrange your thread and scissors in the centre to make sure they'll fit. Mark their positions with your erasable ink pen.

6 Pin then sew the elastic at intervals across the centre of the fabric, looping it slightly over where the thread reels will fit. Cut a 1in (2.5cm) triangle of felt and round off the point; sew this where the point of the scissors will be, leaving the top edge open. Sew the centre of the ribbon in between where the handles of the scissors will fit. Sew a 1in (2.5cm) strip of felt the width of your fabric 1½in (4cm) down from the top. Sew the 6½in (16.5cm) strip centrally, 1in (2.5cm) up from the bottom.

7 On the patchworked side of your work, sew the elastic hair tie to the centre top, facing inwards. My hair tie had a metal section, which I cut off.

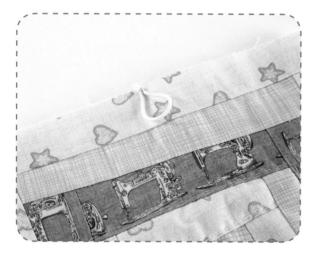

8 Sew the buttons to the 1in (2.5cm) strip of felt – sew them each individually, using separate pieces of thread, as you don't want them all to fall off when you remove just one! Place the two pieces wrong sides together and tack/baste close to the edge. Sew along the two folding lines. Apply the bias binding all around the edge, mitring the corners (see page 16).

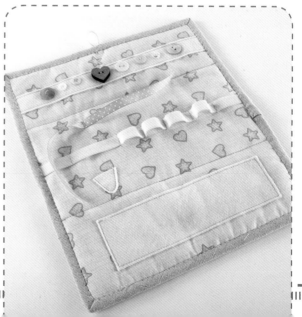

9 Fold the kit and mark the position of the fastening button, then sew in place. Only sew through one layer of the fabric, so that your stitches don't show on the inside.

10 Fill the kit with pins, scissors and thread. Tie the ribbon through the handles of the scissors.

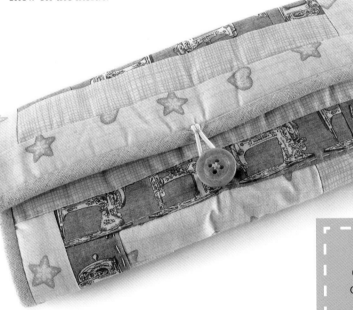

11 Fold over the kit and fasten the button to close.

Pincushion Pot

This handy pot will help you organise small items in your sewing room: pop threads, bobbins and ribbons inside the bowl and stick your pins around the edge!

Finished size

6 x 3in (15.25 x 7.5cm)

What you need

18 x 18in (45.75 x 45.75cm) outer fabric

18 x 18in (45.75 x 45.75cm) lining fabric

3in (7.5cm) circle of card

3in (7.5cm) circle of foam stabiliser

20in (51cm) of ¾in (2cm) wide bias binding

3½oz (100g) toy filler

10in (25.5cm) of 1½in (4cm) wide ribbon tied in a bow

Hand sewing needle and strong thread

Template on page 95

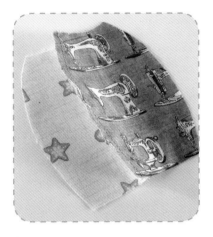 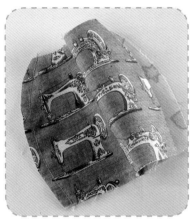

1 Use your template to cut out eight outer fabric shapes and eight lining shapes. Place one outer piece and one lining piece wrong sides together and sew along the left-hand side.

2 With the first two pieces still with wrong sides facing, place a second outer piece right sides together with the first outer piece, and a lining piece right sides together with the first lining. Sew along the right-hand side. Fold the pieces over and press the seam with your fingers.

3 Continue sewing all the pieces together in this way until you have a strip of pockets.

4 Bring the ends of the strip together with the outer pieces facing in. Take the unstitched outer piece and sew right sides together with the first piece that you sewed in step 1. You'll have a complete circle of pockets with one lining piece unsewn.

5 Now you need to sew the lining pieces right sides together. To do this, tightly roll up the circle of pockets between the two unsewn lining edges. Sew the final seam – be careful not to sew through the roll!

6 Pull the fabric from inside this tube and you'll have your full circle of pockets with hidden seams. Trim the top to neaten if necessary, then apply the bias tape around the edge. You'll find it easier to machine sew the tape from the outside of the bowl, then hand sew on the inside.

7 Turn the bowl upside down and stuff each pocket with toy filler.

8 Take a needle and thread and sew a running stitch around the base to close the pockets. Pull the thread to gather until the opening measures 3in (7.5cm).

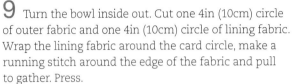

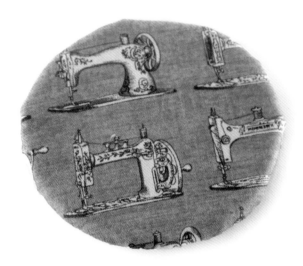

9 Turn the bowl inside out. Cut one 4in (10cm) circle of outer fabric and one 4in (10cm) circle of lining fabric. Wrap the lining fabric around the card circle, make a running stitch around the edge of the fabric and pull to gather. Press.

10 Remove the card, then hand sew to the bottom of the bowl.

11 Turn the bowl right side out. Wrap the outer circle around the foam stabiliser circle and gather; leave the stabiliser in place.

12 Hand sew to the base of the bowl.

13 Sew the bow over the join in the bias binding, and fill your bowl with pins and bobbins!

Tip
This would make a lovely bowl for the dressing table, to keep hair accessories tidy.

Shabby Chic Shoulder Bag

Create a stylish accessory with this relaxed shoulder bag, embellished with beads, buttons and lace, and frayed around the edges. I've used the same fabric for the lining as the outer – as the sides are sewn wrong sides together, the edge of the lining shows through to the outside.

Finished size

14 x 12in (35.5 x 30.5cm), not including strap

What you need

Four 14in (35.5cm) squares of loosely woven fabric: this makes it easier to fray

For the pocket: a piece of the same fabric measuring 9 x 7in (23 x 17.75cm) and a piece of lace measuring 8 x 6in (20.5 x 15.25cm) (you could use several smaller strips)

For the strap: 1½ x 24in (4 x 61cm) length of lace and two lengths of jute trim measuring ½ x 24in (1 x 61cm)

For the bow: 10in (25.5cm) of 1in (2.5cm) wide lace and 8in (20.5cm) of ½in (1cm) wide ribbon

For the flower: 40 x 3in (101.75 x 10cm) fabric and a bead to decorate the centre, 10in (25.5cm) pearl bead trim, 10 x 1in (25.5 x 2.5cm) frayed fabric

Six buttons: or use as many as you like!

To trim the straps: 40in (101.75cm) of 1½in (4cm) wide lace; 40in (101.75cm) of 2in (5cm) wide lace; 40in (101.75cm) of ¼in (5mm) wide ribbon; 30in (76cm) pearl bead trim; 20in (51cm) string

Magnetic clasp

Extra fabric scraps

Erasable ink pen

Ruler

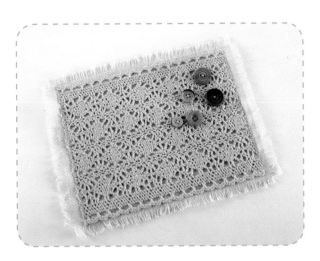

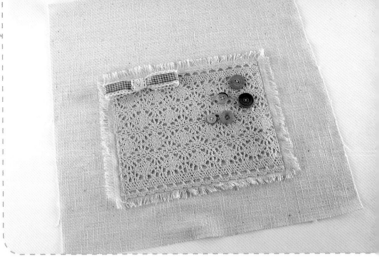

1 Fray ½in (1cm) around the edge of the pocket fabric. Place the wide lace over the top and satin stitch around the edge. Hand sew on five of the buttons in a random arrangement.

2 Make up the bow by placing 8in (20.5cm) of the ribbon on top of 8in (20.5cm) of lace, fold into a loop and sew the ends together. Wrap the remaining lace around the centre and sew, then hand sew the bow onto the pocket. Place the pocket centrally over one of the large squares, 2in (5cm) up from the bottom. Sew around three sides leaving the top open.

3 Take the two squares of fabric that will become the lining and apply a magnetic clasp piece centrally to each, 3½in (9cm) from the top. Place a square of extra fabric behind the clasps to stop the prongs pulling through when you're opening the bag.

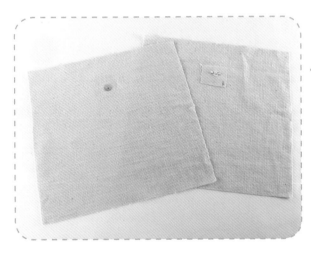

4 Place each lining piece wrong sides together with an outer piece. Measure 1in (2.5cm) from the top of the outer pieces and draw a line with your erasable ink pen. Measure and mark the sides 1in (2.5cm) below these lines. Sew across the top line through both layers of fabric with a small stitch – this will stop the fabric fraying more than you want it to.

5 With the lined front and back pieces wrong sides together and the magnetic clasp fastened, sew with a small stitch 1in (2.5cm) from the edge, between the two marks at the sides of the fabric. This will form two flaps at the top of the bag.

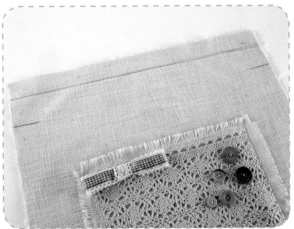

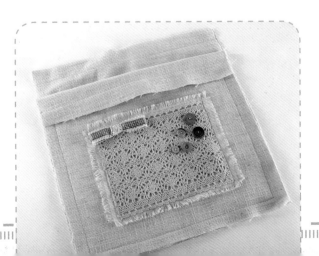

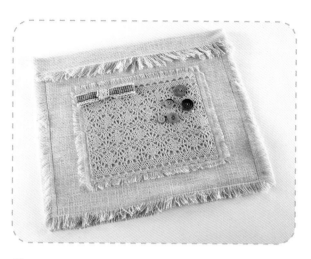

6 Now for the fun bit: fray the edges of all four layers of fabric to create a 1in (2.5cm) fringe all the way around the bag.

7 Sew the jute trim to either side of the lace to make the strap.

8 Part the fringing at the sides of the bag, fold the ends of the strap under by ½in (1cm) and sew to each side. Cut the ribbon, lace, bead trim and string in half. Tie each half together with the string pieces.

9 Tie these to the base of the strap either side of the bag using the string to knot them. Sew the final button – mine is a heart shape – to the top of the bag. Make up the flower in the same way as for the letter holder on page 42. Fold the frayed strip of fabric and bead trim in half and sew to the bag, then sew the flower on top.

Tip
My fabric is quite heavy – if you're using linen or cotton you may wish to use wadding/batting to make it a little more sturdy.

Templates

All the templates are given at actual size. Simply trace them off and cut them out. The heart and the posy cone template should each be mirrored along the dashed line.

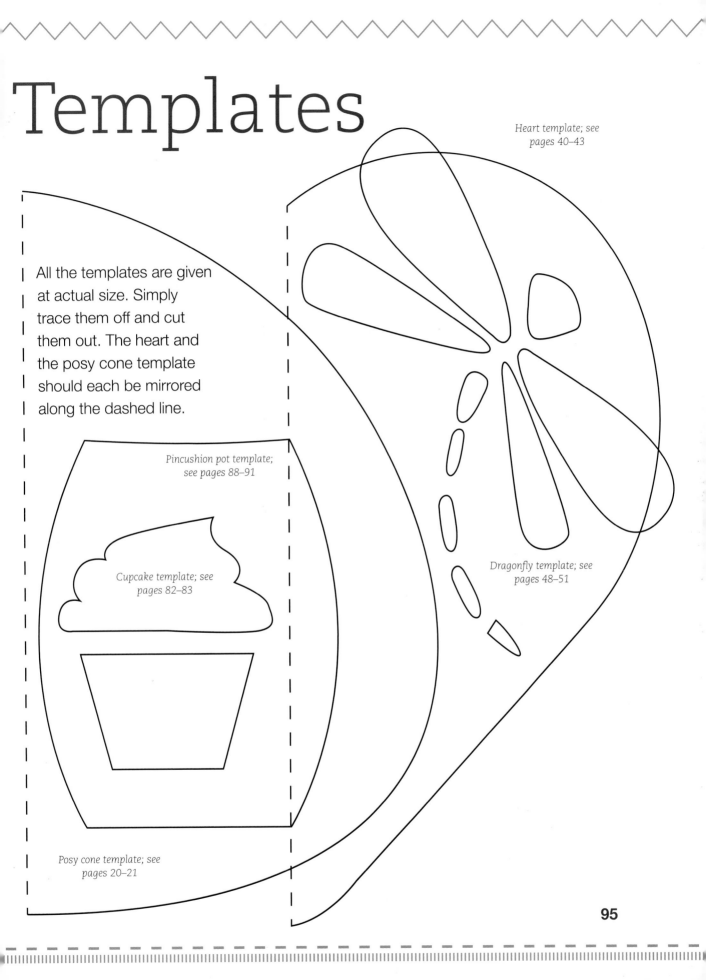

Heart template; see pages 40–43

Pincushion pot template; see pages 88–91

Cupcake template; see pages 82–83

Dragonfly template; see pages 48–51

Posy cone template; see pages 20–21

Index